LOVE YOUR WORK AND MAKE MORE MONEY

Advance Praise

"Honest and inspirational. Ideal for women who aspire to achieve more but aren't sure how to get there."

— **Jill Konrath**, Author of *More Sales Less Time* and *SNAP Selling*

"If you're seeking the motivation to be fearless in pursuing your career goals, read this book."

— **Amir Husain**, Founder & CEO, SparkCognition

"Jenny Krengel is a masterful storyteller.

"The 8 Truths she introduces in this book are practical, real, and move you forward quickly. For any woman looking to make a shift in her life, this compelling author will walk you through precisely what you need to do to love your work."

— **Ramona Arora**, Ph.D., Lecturer and Career Coach, University of Texas at Austin, McCombs School of Business. Consultant, Talent and Culture Center of Excellence. Dell Technologies

"I believe this book is valuable for anyone, regardless of gender or journey. Jenny's authenticity is inspiring and instructional. Be prepared to take action within a framework that is truly illuminating.

"This book will guide the way with practical examples, powerful testimony, and clear steps for creating a life driven by purpose, delivering fulfillment and success."

— **Maxwell Dodge**, VP of Business Development, Kudelski Security

LOVE YOUR WORK
AND
MAKE MORE MONEY

*Unleash Your 8 Truths
to Connect with the
Work You are Meant to Do*

JENNY KRENGEL

NEW YORK

LONDON • NASHVILLE • MELBOURNE • VANCOUVER

LOVE YOUR WORK AND MAKE MORE MONEY
Unleash Your 8 Truths to Connect with the Work You are Meant to Do

© 2018 **JENNY KRENGEL**

Published in New York, New York, by Morgan James Publishing in partnership with Difference Press. Morgan James is a trademark of Morgan James, LLC. www.MorganJamesPublishing.com

The Morgan James Speakers Group can bring authors to your live event. For more information or to book an event visit The Morgan James Speakers Group at www.TheMorganJamesSpeakersGroup.com.

ISBN 978-1-68350-807-6 paperback
ISBN 978-1-68350-808-3 eBook
Library of Congress Control Number: 2017915975

Cover Design by:
Rachel Lopez
www.r2cdesign.com

Interior Design by:
Bonnie Bushman
The Whole Caboodle Graphic Design

In an effort to support local communities, raise awareness and funds, Morgan James Publishing donates a percentage of all book sales for the life of each book to Habitat for Humanity Peninsula and Greater Williamsburg.

Get involved today! Visit
www.MorganJamesBuilds.com

DEDICATION

For my daughter, Lily:
What can I show you, what can
I teach you, what can I leave you?
My experiences, stories, and my love;
it's all I have that is mine, and all that matters in life.
May *you* live a life of being fearless…
making your own stories extraordinary.

In memory of Christi Lanahan:
Twenty years was not enough of you on this earth.
While I will never do the task justice,
I endeavor to live enough life for the both of us.

TABLE OF CONTENTS

INTRODUCTION

Erin is fiercely loyal.

Loyal to her boss, loyal to her co-workers, loyal to her friends, loyal to her family, and even loyal to strangers because she has a volunteer's heart. She learned to be loyal because it is the honorable way to live a life. Put others first. It is what is right, and it is what is good. Erin learned these beliefs from her church and her parents and a society that tells her the proper way to be a woman. Erin is loyal to everyone—except herself.

At work she tells herself, "*Don't speak up, you might upset someone. Put your head down, work hard, and don't say too much, because telling someone how you feel and what you want might be stupid. Don't show your weaknesses. What I want doesn't really* matter, or it can wait. I just need to do my job, and it will be okay. I should be grateful to even have a job."

Erin is great at keeping secrets because she learned so many, growing up. When she keeps her secrets, she becomes the perfect person. The perfect sister, daughter, employee, and someday… a perfect wife and mother.

But she feels empty, different, and lonely, even when she is with her friends. When she gets angry over anything, she can't find the words to express herself, and she just wants to cry… out of frustration. Erin feels different because everyone else's life seems so happy. Everyone has it all together, except her. She often asks herself, "*What the f* is wrong with me?*"

When chaos breaks out, Erin is phenomenal. Remember, she is loyal. She is the one who is ultra-responsible. She can fix anything and make everything seem perfect. Her siblings get tired of her "angel child" syndrome. Mom's favorite.

Going on auto-pilot and staying on the hamster wheel feels most comfortable to Erin. *Don't ruffle any feathers.* If she keeps super busy, she won't have to sit with how she *really* feels. Insecure. Unsure. The hamster wheel is predictable, yet after a while it is boring. It's also covered in s***.

Erin is not a big drinker or partier, so she doesn't stir up chaos that way, nor is she is promiscuous. But after a while, she will look for someone else to serve, or find some*one* who will be a great project. Then she will get sucked dry. Again.

Her brain is conditioned to doubt herself, to fix things, and to take care of everyone else first. She forgets about her dreams. She searches for something different in her life by way of yoga, an occasional retreat, and spending time alone reading books, but nothing is really working yet. She's unmarried, yet whatever it is her man wants to do, she's up for it.

There have been turbulent times at work, and her boss is inconsistent. Some days are unbearable, but Erin talks herself into everything being okay. *I'll just settle here. The money is okay. I don't need that much.* She believes this story *again*, and another day goes by with Erin being soul-sucked at work.

One day, on Facebook, Erin saw an offer to learn my secret sauce to fearlessly loving your work and reached out to me. She was looking for a female mentor in business. She has a small network, and spends time socializing, but has been ineffective in being able to articulate what it is she wants next in her career.

The common theme for her has been jumping from one toxic environment to the next: feeling undervalued and making limited money. Not making enough money to meet her financial goals. Not making enough money to pamper herself and get the occasional massage she craves and needs. Empty inside. Empty bank account. She tells me she wants change, and to "make her way out." During my vetting process, she had to tell me why she had grit, and she did so, with ease. We began to work together.

Then one morning, about six months later Erin wakes up, and the hamster wheel is gone. She is challenged to approach her day differently. There is a giant purpose in her life now, and all roads lead to that exciting destination! All of a sudden, she is not rushed or overwhelmed; she feels completely at peace, and nothing can lure her to over-perform. Erin is making twice as much money now, and she has planned her dream vacation with her man! Her new employer is taking out extra money for her 401K (which they match), and the savings account for her niece's and nephew's study abroad is nearing its goal! She went to work for a start-up that gave her some stock options, and the company's revenue growth is off the charts.

At the end of the work day, her boss asks her to do something before she leaves, but she kindly tells him she has plans for the evening and has to leave (her only plans were to get home when she was ready to leave the office); she will get to that last request first thing in the morning. Her boss apologizes for making such a ridiculous request so late in the day, and tells her to have a fabulous evening because work can always wait. The next day is Wednesday, and she can't wait for her scheduled day to be working from home!

What is different for Erin? How has this new person appeared? How did she shift her priorities and mindset? Who is this boss? Nothing seems to rattle Erin like before, and she is living with complete joy at work, and in her personal life. The days of overwhelm and doubt are over.

Like Dorothy in the Wizard of Oz, who always had a way home through her ruby slippers, Erin has all her answers. But she needed me. She needed my help to sort out all the dirty laundry and to start fresh.

When I decided to get back to basics, "embrace my crazy," and let my talents and values unfold for me, I returned to the work I was put on this earth to do. In my career I've made mistakes, and I've had wild success.

This book will give you 8 Truths to uncover and live by. They are truths because they are yours. You will learn the step-by-step discovery process to create a career and work-life that is fulfilling and meaningful. This book contains what you need to be like Erin. You will either love your work and make more money, or, if money is not an issue for you because you have alternative income, *at least you will love your work.* The 8 Truths are divided into three main parts: Being Aware, Being Active, and Being Assertive. Once you have found your compass in the truths, I will have given you a practical roadmap to put those truths into play.

May you keep your dreams big, find your path sooner, trust yourself and the process, and keep your eyes on the prize ahead. That's the only direction that matters; looking back on the past only slows us down and can keep us in a negative pattern.

You gotta decide what you want for the right reasons. Then go do it.

This life we live is a flash. There is no time to waste, and no time to spend waiting.

No time to be waiting on that dream job, waiting on finances to change, or waiting for that vacation that keeps screaming your name… the time is now. Now is when you have to decide that you want your life to be different.

In this country, it is a beautiful thing to know… that deep in your heart, the only thing in your way to the life you really want is you and your bag of beliefs.

Turn off the past noise from your mom. Turn off the past noise from your dad. Turn off the past noise and hurts from every boss, teacher, boyfriend, girlfriend, bully, Facebook post, Tweet, and Instagram image.

Turn *on your light*, because it is waiting to laser cut its way to what *you* want.

Try. Try again. Refine. Try again. Every step ahead, and every step back, *is a step.*

And each step brings you closer to Planet Marvelous.

Make your time here matter by *being fearless.* It's showtime!

All my love and support for your journey,

Jenny

HOW BEING FEARLESS SAVED ME

———∾∾———

"The world needs dreamers and the world needs doers.
But above all the world needs dreamers who do."
–Sarah Ban Breathnach

I believe your Truths will set you free.

In 2014, my job world and personal world collided in chaos, and all I wanted was to feel joy again, and to feel free. I *had* to do what mattered again, so I began the process of finding my way back to my Truths to get my life back on track. A process I had done many times over my curvaceous career.

Here is what I know about myself and my career. Both are messy, and neither has made a lot of sense. Some might call it, "all over the place," or maybe, "non-traditional." That is my spirit in a nutshell. Clearly a non-linear path, but a wonderful and mysterious path that has been filled with adventure, taking risks, learning a ton about business, having fun, working with wicked-smart people, *and* the bonus of making *lots* of money on a flexible schedule!

My track record shows I fearlessly tried things, and my customers will tell you I care to the nth degree. I care about people, I see *possibility in things and people*, and I care about results because I take pride in my work.

A master of making myself feel better—or self-soothing— by creating, performing, producing, and delivering, these are skills with which I have been blessed and cursed. I've realized that I will give, give, give until I break. I have this superpower, for which I am most grateful, of drive and determination that originated as a result of a chaotic, dysfunctional household as a child. I am comfortable with uncertainty, and I've discovered that this finely honed skill serves me well in start- ups and relocating!

Almost my entire life, I couldn't understand why I've always felt different, and why I felt like something was missing. Until now.

Fearless Early On:

As far back as I can remember, I had this fearless fire in my belly to *do* stuff. I would try almost anything that might be fun.

The first time I remember feeling fearless was when I was about six years old. We lived in a small house on a small hill. When you went down our hill, the road turned left or right, and if you went straight, you would be at the front door of a neighbor's house. With limited, if any, experience on a bike, I decided my big brother's bicycle would make a fun downhill run. As the "T" in the road at the bottom of the hill approached, I suddenly realized my bare feet could not reach the brake pedals. I ended up crashing into the neighbor's front door; all the while my mother was running behind in her nightgown, and my brother was taking big strides alongside me, trying to make the rescue.

I don't remember the crash hurting or even being scary, but I do remember thinking, "Wow, that was a fun run downhill!"

As a kid, I was the short scrappy girl stealing the basketball, and the softball player who ran the bases with wild abandon.

Somehow I had this extra gear where I would shift into fearlessness when I made up my mind to go for it. And I still have it.

I've figured out that when I am in alignment with my dreams and my values, familiar with myself, who I am and what I want, I am fearless.

Being Fearless in My Career:

My 20s—Financial Survival: Your 20s are a fantastic time to be wide-eyed, curious, and fearless when it comes to work. Young enough to still be naive and get some free passes on the dumb-tax, yet old enough *not* to be a completely clueless idiot. It helps if you have parents who have money, but I did not.

When I was 23 years old, I was living in Austin, Texas, working as a dance instructor in a studio, and as a waitress at the first and only Chuy's location, on Barton Springs Blvd. At the time, I was a college drop-out and—having never taken permanent residency in any other place on the planet—I wanted to move to Dallas to live in the big city. I was ready for an adventure!

Scouring the want-ads, I found a telecom services company that was hiring a receptionist. I called the number, passed an interview over the phone, and then was hired. I was moving to Dallas with a big car payment and a small dog named Cocky! Looking back, my mom must have thought I was insane to pick up and leave, but she did not stop me. She knew I needed to go. After I got there, I figured out that working as a receptionist making $16,000 a year was not going to cut it.

That salary was not going to finance the big dreams I had for myself, much less my apartment rent in Irving, my outrageous car payment of $350/mo, and maybe some fancy shoes from Foley's instead of Pay-Less. As I grew up, mom struggled insanely on a school teacher's salary to support three kids and my dad, so it would have been the natural progression to unconsciously put my adult self in the same chaotic financial pattern.

But I wanted something different for my life.

Before apps, there were these contraptions called calculators. I actually had an electric-powered calculator with a paper tape roll at my desk to add up the accounts receivable checks. I mastered the art of not looking at the calculator while my right hand whizzed through the clicks, just like the lady at the bank! I thought I was really talented and the sound was so impressive—especially the amplified noise from the acrylic fake nails I had at the time that I could not afford.

My mobile calculator was a 3" x 5" solar-powered model, so half the time it would not work, but one place it would *always* work was under the fluorescent light at the Kroger store in Irving. I would add up the groceries in my basket as I shopped, hoping I had added everything correctly. I did not want to return a batch of celery to the checker.

One day I told myself, "The day I don't bring my calculator to the grocery store is the day I will be *rich*!"

So I moved to another office-girl job making a whopping $18,000 a year, and about a year into that gig, I decided I wanted to try Sales! The company was Toner Cartridge Services (TCS), and they were green before green was cool. They were in the business of remanufacturing (recycling) toner cartridges, and servicing laser printers.

Now this was *not* a sexy product, but the thought of selling anything was my way out of being stuck in an office all day, being in a reactive role and having no control over my time or my income. I knew the customers, the product, the operation, and anything having to do with the back office.

I mustered my courage, and slowly walked to the VP of Sales' small office in the back of the building, starkly adorned with his EE degree from Texas A&M on the wall. In memory, he was a nervous kind of guy, anxious, never really calm, but smart as a whip, and nice.

Sheepishly standing in his door I asked, "Jim, I think I am ready to go into sales. May I try?"

He says to me, "No, I think you are more valuable here in the office. We need you answering the phones and doing all the other stuff. You're the only one who knows where everything is."

I heard the word "valuable," so *that* was good. But I was rejected. The hopes for myself and my new adventure were put to rest, and I went about my day, but I felt like I had been punched in the gut. I wanted to try something new, but while he did not use the words to say it, he told me he did not believe in me. Jim is a good person, and in that moment he was rushed, and not engaged, or thinking about what was important to me, as a loyal employee.

It goes to show what an impact leadership has on the confidence of capable people, if the leader does not take the time to understand. I kept my head down and remembered the Abe Lincoln quote, "Whatever you are, be a good one." I continued to be the best "office girl" possible, and continued to watch, learn, and hone my skills about the customers, the product, and the operation.

About six to eight months later, I regained the courage to make the request again. While I believe fully in following chain of command, this time I went to the co-founder and President to make my plea. I walked a little taller and spoke a little braver and announced in his doorway, "I want to try Sales." He was wearing a yellow button-down Oxford, and looked up from his work, smiled broadly, and said, "I think you will be great! *Just be yourself.*"

From that moment on, I had someone who believed in me and my ability to be a successful sales lady. I sold millions of dollars' worth of TCS products and services to enterprise (large company) accounts, and was a key contributor in growing the business for a run of almost nine years. Jim was long gone for other reasons, but I became the sales leader.

The "no" that I got from Jim was another gift in disguise. Overcoming a major objection played out in real life before me, and it was my first lesson in understanding what sales is. What if I had listened to my first "no"? I quickly discovered that overcoming objections was a natural process, and a natural gift I had because of my vision for myself.

Early 30s—*Finally* Putting Myself First: At 31 years old, I wanted a personal life. I had spent almost nine years pouring my heart and soul into someone else's dream (surprise!), and I could see my role at TCS was not going to give me what I wanted out of life. Leaving this company was an emotional divorce for me. I loved my family there. But with the help of therapy and determination, I got the strength to love myself more.

I had just hit the six-figure mark being a sales leader for a $15M company that I helped grow, and I announced to the CEO I was planning to go back to school to finish my college degree. I was giving nine months' notice. The break-up was slow and painful at times, and I don't think I would recommend that much pre-planning, but I wanted to feel like I was taking care of the people I loved by not just leaving abruptly.

An admissions visit to the Dean at the University of Texas at Dallas was funny. I was interviewing him and making my decision about going back to school, and he says to me, "Let me get this straight. Most people go to school so they can earn six-figures. You want to leave a six-figure job to go back to school?"

"Yes, sir. "

And I was off to the races.

When I left TCS to finish my education, I only knew three things:

1. Finishing college was important to me.
2. I was fascinated by Psychology.
3. I was debt-free because I planned for this moment, but I lived by myself, had no financial support, and I would have to take out a student loan to pay for school.

Before my student loan was approved, I had to get a job. And I needed flexibility. What kind of job offers that to students? Being a waitress, of course.

Houston's Restaurant hired me, and there I was, in my white apron, white button-down shirt, black pants, and my first pair of Doc Martens. Then my student loan came through, and we are still paying it off today, 20 years later. 0% interest, so why not?

Graduating with honors was one of my proudest moments, at 32 years old. I had a formal education, a business education, and now I was on the loose!

After graduation, I spent some time in graduate work, but theory was not for me. I liked to apply my skills, and make things happen!

I spent the next few years in management and selling again. I worked in start-ups except for one company which had only 1500 employees. I always liked to feel like I was making a difference and had some control over outcomes. I never felt like I could do that or make any significant impact for a large company.

Mid 30s—Fearless Fun:

Don't ever ignore your third base coach when he tells you *not* to go. The day after running the Capitol 10K, I had a co-ed softball game with my co-workers. My muscles were cramping but it was a perfect Spring night and a great time with friends. My streak of fearlessness backfired this time. I was sprinting to third base, and the coach had his arms up shouting, "Hold up! Hold up!" I had full momentum, and like the third-grade base runner with pigtails flying, I went for it anyway. Pushing the limit. Always the dare-devil. I knew the ball was coming in behind me, so I was going to slide like I had done countless times before. But this time my left cleat stuck. It stuck hard as I went in for the right-leg-first slide. My body went, but the left ankle was planted. I went dizzy, could not move, and all I remember is the umpire just wanting me off his base. For the record, I was safe and it was the game tying run… I always know the score so that's probably why I went anyway.

With a new a metal plate and seven screws in my ankle, almost a year in a cast, and living by myself on crutches with way too much time on my hands, I crafted my next career move.

I was going to apply for the FBI.

This interview was 14 months long. No process for any job has given me more insight and growth. I was pushed to limits I did not know I had. Both emotionally and physically. Along the way, I was asked two life-changing questions: What is the worst thing that has ever happened to you? What is the best thing that has ever happened to you?

It occurred to me the answer was the same, and this realization changed my life.

It was the day my roommate Christi and I were run over by a drunk driver. She was dragged 800 feet and killed, and somehow I was spared. *This* fact was something so horrible and unimaginable. Yet the moment I realized I was left here to live a full and meaningful life, and that every moment is an opportunity to thrive, my mind was blown.

The FBI did not hire me. I took four polygraph tests which were all inconclusive because my hands didn't sweat, and they told me I controlled my breathing. (I was a runner at the time.) The polygraph examiner called me on a regular basis and took me to dinner one night. He was married and in no uncertain terms wanted to sleep with me. I did not participate with him, but in retrospect his actions were clearly sexual harassment. He called me after I received my confusing rejection letter (after I had already received an invitation to go to new hire training at Quantico), and he told me I was "too bright of a star" for the FBI. He said he felt like I would be too constrained by all the bureaucracy and that I should be somewhere where I could make a difference.

He was right. But my fantasy of being an agent was crushed.

Late 30s—A Targeted Vision:

Since the FBI did not want me, I wanted to figure out a way to combine my technical skills in selling software and hardware with the idea of catching bad guys—white collar criminals. So I was back at the research game.

I knew what I wanted. I had a vision for my life: to love my work so I could buy my first home! What could be better?

Through my exhaustive research, I found a private company in California that was selling computer forensics software.

Bingo! That was it. I contacted HR and told them why they should hire me, but they did not have an enterprise product yet. (An enterprise product is a product that large companies use system-wide. In the software world, these purchases are complex and expensive.) HR told me the product would not be out for about six months. So I called, and called, and called, and emailed and emailed. I finally got an interview, and I was hired as the first sales rep in Texas, covering a five-state territory. My boss was the best. He believed in me, and expected a lot from me. I did 15 deals in 18 months in a green-field territory where there was almost no installed base. He called me the "Texas Tornado." I loved that job and it showed.

I got married during the process, then got a boss who micro-managed the performers, and I got pregnant. It was a cocktail for quitting, so I did. The company replaced my role with three people, and the sales rep who inherited my deals was the top performing rep for the company for several years following.

The 40s—Time for Flight:

After I had my daughter, I chose to stay home with her for the first year. During that year, I was feeling restless and guilty. *Why am I not enjoying being a stay-at-home mom?* I thought I could do some part-time work, but in a professional setting. I didn't want to sell skin care products or have any part of any multi-level marketing, high-pressure sales gig. I wanted to use my valuable skills in a part-time or flexible work arrangement.

I couldn't find anything out there, so I decided to start a business. It would be a software company that helps women return to the workforce after having children. I would call it Dream Jobs Inc.

Fast forward four years and we had some local, paying customers, but we had pivoted to serve large companies in financial services who had built programs to support their diversity efforts to bring back highly educated, skilled, and trained women to the workforce.

We were working diligently on beta programs with Goldman Sachs and Lehman Brothers, and it was the fall of 2009. Then everything came crashing down. I had to close the business, and it broke my heart.

So, forever the problem solver and re-inventor, I went back to a former employer, killed it again in B2B high tech sales (this skill sticks for life and will never leave you), and life was back to what I knew. But my dream had been crushed, and at the time I didn't realize I had lost my fire, but in reality it took me seven years to get my confidence back.

Today: We hear about being "passionate" about what we do. So looking back on those defining moments, I wanted to figure out how I got "passionate" about selling a commoditized consumable product that was technically before its time, and what made me believe so fiercely in a myriad of software applications. Now I know the answer. I had a vision for a better life and a purpose, and I believed in the products and companies I worked for. In my 20s, my purpose was to find financial relief and a way out, and that purpose bred a drive in me. I was grateful just for being alive, and did not want to waste a minute.

My definition of being rich by not taking a calculator to the store is a low bar, but it was a bar that was necessary, and one I do not forget or take for granted. Based on my temporary definition of rich, I have been rich for decades. I regularly remind myself of that to appreciate what I have earned, and to put things into perspective. Keep setting goals for yourself because, as you attain them, you can raise the bar or change the definition.

Small steps toward something different can pay huge dividends when your purpose is clear, you persevere, and the right people believe in you. Confidence comes through action. Now what do you need to do? Once you identify and integrate *your* truths, you will begin to feel instant relief and hope for a brighter future that you decide to build!

Action: Buy a beautiful journal. Don't cheap out. Make it mean something to you.

For the first entry, notate the date and answer these two questions:

1. When have I been fearless, and what were my results?
2. What am I most proud of?

This journal is your gratitude journal. Every night before bed, write down three things for which you are grateful. (It is impossible to be angry and grateful simultaneously.)

THE 8 TRUTHS YOU MUST KNOW

―――∾∾∾――――

"This above all; to thine own self be true."
– William Shakespeare

Who doesn't want to love their work? Work can be fun, fulfilling, meaningful, and financially rewarding when we are aligned with what we *really* want. Not what mom wants, not what dad wants, and most certainly not what we *think* we should do because society tells us so.

Everywhere you turn, on Facebook or in articles that pop up on your screen when you are trying to work, there are ads touting how to become rich by being an entrepreneur. For the record, I'd love it if people would stop using the term "mompreneur." No one uses the term "dadpreneur," so please stop. This alternative term reiterates gender *differences*, and I think we all serve ourselves better by identifying our similarities. (One is either an entrepreneur or not.) The other messages we see on a daily basis are, "Escape corporate America! Work for yourself! Find your passion!"

There is an allure to these messages, I know, because I have lived some of them.

My message to you is that not everyone is meant to be an entrepreneur, and if you are, expertise helps. You get expertise through life and work experience. Sure, there are success anomalies. There are brilliant people with brilliant ideas who have perfect timing and an awesome product. There are those who have parents or spouses with financial backing, and phenomenal networks because Mom or Dad knows someone who is the on the board somewhere. I believe in going after dreams and thinking big, but don't ever tell yourself being an entrepreneur is easy.

Here is the message I believe women need to hear: Working in corporate America can be awesome! Sure, there are crappy cultures and crappy people to work for, but there are more cultures and people that are fantastic, than are f'd up. Working for start-ups is the best gift I was ever given. Working for smaller companies gave me my wings and experience *to become* an entrepreneur. Smaller companies *let you be you*. You *get* the privilege to wear many hats, try them all on, and figure out which one fits best.

If you find yourself in a crappy job, why did you take the job to begin with? Better yet, why are you staying? The answers to those questions really have more to do with you than your employer. It's no one's fault you are working there, getting a paycheck, and providing service, except yours. When you feel frustrated, under-valued, and upset on a daily basis, it is time to look at what you can do differently, because then you are in the driver's seat.

So you took a class on writing the perfect resume? You've sat through webinars telling you how to triple your income in three months. You've networked in LinkedIn. You've spent hours applying on-line for jobs. Maybe you are content where you are, but do you know you can do better?

Over the course of decades, I've seen hundreds of resumes from people who are looking for a job.

Typically my first question is, "What is it you want to do, and why?"

And why? That's the stumper.

Usually the answer has a twinge of ambiguity with a sprinkle of generality. Throw in a dash of doubt. I'm usually blown away by the lack of clarity. If the person is employed and they are unhappy, I am always curious about the root cause.

A job is like any personal relationship. When things get bad and you leave, life does not necessarily get better. It is when we realize what we are (and what we are not) willing to tolerate that a shift can occur. The truth is, patterns repeat themselves until the common denominator changes. Perhaps it is time to hold the mirror up? *Prior to even considering* a job search or change—which may likely lead to the next frying pan—there are 8 Truths you must be clear about. Once you are, the process becomes magical.

1. Beliefs: These are rules we have learned, either from our childhood, from experience, or by making interesting assumptions that may or may not be true. There are two types of beliefs—living beliefs and disabling beliefs. Disabling beliefs hold us back, and living beliefs are those that let us fly. For example, a disabling belief may be, "I'm too young; no one would ever hire me to do that job." A living belief may be, "Age is just a number—I'm going for it!"

2. Values: Our heart's desire for how we want to live our life. What is *truly* important in order to live our lives with joy and abundance? Values are either fear-based or consciousness-based. For example, a fear-based value would be "Accomplishment." You see, accomplishment depends on external forces. There is some kind of comparison to be able to identify what accomplishment is, and it relies on a competing force. A consciousness-based value would be "Integrity." Integrity is something you have complete control over, and it does not depend on any external force. A good test for values is to ask yourself if they would hold up and would serve you on a desert island, where the only person you could depend on would be yourself.

3. Vision: We hear about vision statements, and blah, blah, blah. But a vision can present itself by asking yourself, "What do I want? What does my life look like in x years?" When working with clients, I like to use three years as a good baseline for vision work. It's not the, "If you were on your deathbed at 100 years old,

what would you regret not doing?" exercise, but it is a practical and attainable way to dream big, in a realistic chunk of time. This is the moment to dream, and to picture the ideal scenario. Your vision is an outcome. If you are not willing to go there, then you will stay on the hamster wheel, knee-deep in poop.

4. Purpose: Purpose is not something to be chased. "Purpose" is a single word for "What's the point?" Your purpose is a verb linked to your vision. For example, if my purpose is "to fund experiences for myself and others," my behaviors or activities in life drive me to run a profitable business, which ties to my vision of living anywhere in the world. See how this works? Your purpose can change. It depends on how big you want to make your vision, and you can have several. I currently have four that I love, feel entirely connected to, and that have been solid for six months. I do not see them changing for years, although I may add to the list.

5. Commitment: What are the activities you are willing to commit to daily, weekly, monthly, and yearly to achieve your purpose? For example, *I am committed to living authentically, taking action, and developing talent because my purpose is to inspire others to live into their potential.* If I am ever feeling confused about what I need to "get done" in a day, I look to my left where my single sheet of my Vision, Purpose, and Commitment statements are hung, and I get completely on track! These statements are guides,

roadmaps—whatever you want to call them—they work, and they will keep you aligned.

6. Criteria: This one is interesting. I say that, because when I ask the question, "What is most important to you in your next job?" there is usually a long pause. Clearly knowing and articulating the criteria for a career or job is critical. Examples of criteria may be: short commute, engaged boss, private workspace—you get it. The list is subjective because you are the only judge of what the criteria means *to you*. Many years ago, I had four job offers, and I was completely confused about which job to take. I was not clear about my criteria. So I invented a tool and a system to evaluate which job offer to take. It was like magic!

7. Differentiators: This key component comes into play when you are networking, or prospecting the recruiters to get an interview, and it is *really* important to know when you are in front of the decision maker. (Who, by the way, is rarely the recruiter. The recruiter can play an important role in the gate-keeping process, but there are differences in how you approach the recruiter vs. the hiring manager.) How are you going to differentiate yourself? Remember, *you* are the product. Do you have a way to make yourself memorable?

8. Negotiating position: If you are clear on the seven previous steps, the chances of a job offer—or multiple job offers—is highly likely. The most powerful person in a negotiation is the one who has crystal

clear clarity on what they want and why. I cannot stress this concept enough. The one who knows their position is the one who succeeds in achieving what they set out to do.

When it comes to a job or career, for good reason the emphasis is on skills, training, and education. Most people search for a "job," and I am suggesting you search for a place where you can give your gifts, skills, and talents that *align* with what it is you want for your life. Sometimes grit can go a lot farther than a sterile degree, and it's possible for a driven, motivated receptionist to outplay the polished greed-mongering-bully in a sales contest.

My Why

There are two questions I asked myself that serve as the inspiration for this book:

1. "Jenny: What *don't* you know?"

Of course I don't know Russian, how to program anything worthwhile, the Chinese alphabet, advanced math, or the majority of accounting principles. There are obvious facts and skills I do not know or ever wish to know.

What don't you know about yourself? I found my answer quickly:

I don't know my potential.

When things get hard, or I choose to be "overwhelmed," I will talk myself into mediocrity. I *feel* uncomfortable, so I let myself off the hook by making up some story in my head about how I am not good enough, or smart enough, or capable enough, or whatever bulls*** line I can come up with. I decided that I love it when my eyes light up and my speech pattern increases when I get excited about helping other women step into their potential. I believe we all vastly underestimate our gifts, so I want to pull the best out of you, and I know how! This insight leads us to the next question I asked myself:

2. How do I wrap Jenny up, put a bow on it, and share what I've learned in my career? I was curious about how I could package my sales philosophy to teach women how to sell anything. And remember, inventing or reinventing yourself for a career or job *is* selling yourself.

My personal approach to sales throughout my 25-year career happens to fit nicely into the Golden Circle which Simon Sinek introduced to the world in 2009. I've always had my process, and after I read his book, I finally felt like I had real validation. And it was from someone who was really smart! I applied the three rings to what I knew to be true for myself, and voila, I had my Sales Mastery Model™. Let me take you through the model. I've adapted it to apply to a career search.

~~Sales~~ Career Mastery Model™

Think of a traditional job search as a three-layer cake. The bottom of the cake is the biggest, in terms of time and the relative amount of training, information, or noise that is in the marketplace. It contains all the activities and tasks for *how* to find a job. Most often, this is the area of focus where people start their job search. Normal tasks include: researching, networking, applying, creating resumes, managing time, and interviewing. If you were looking at this three-layer cake from the top down, the base of the cake would be the outer ring, what I call "the edge."

The middle layer would relate to *what* job you want, and *who* you want to work for. This area is similar to a marketing function in an organization. For example, marketing is responsible for product definition (that would be you in a job search), targeting the customer (employer), and understanding the competitive advantages. The middle ring of the model is what I call "the center."

Lastly, the cake topper, or what I call "the core" of the model. This is the most beautiful part of the cake, and it is personal. This part of the cake can sit atop any other cake and make it distinct and personal and beautiful. At a special event, this part of the cake is preserved to enjoy again and celebrate something wonderful. This part of the model is where the 8 Truths live.

The core is your personal *why*.

Getting to the Work

Putting the Career Mastery Model™ to use:

In sales, the edge would be: *How* to Sell. Tasks and activities include researching, prospecting, networking, presenting, proposing, and negotiating.

In a job search, the edge would be: *How* to Find a Job: researching, prospecting, networking, presenting (resume), proposing (interview), and negotiating (job offer).

In sales, the center would be: *What* I am selling, and to *whom*. This is marketing's job. Activities in the center include product definition, pricing, competitive advantage, and who will buy this product?

In a job search, the center would be: *What* company do I want to work for? *Who* will hire me and why? *Who* is my competition?

In sales, the core would be: Who I am, and why I sell.

In a job search, the core would be: Who I am and what do I want? My why.

We are flipping the job search model and starting from the inside out. This is where we start, and it will be your peace of mind, your compass, and your heart.

This innovative book will teach you the 8 Truths to know *before* searching for a new job, role, or career, and before making any change in a job, role, or career.

The word fearless happens to have eight letters, and I wanted to avoid spelling anything out, but it just so works out:

The 8 TRUTHS *build in this order:* F-E-A-R-L-E-S-S

#1 Fix Your *Beliefs*—How the beliefs we learn and develop impact our personal interactions. Our beliefs about money have unbelievable power over our behavior at work.

#2 Embody *Values*—How are you identifying and aligning with your heart's desire for how you want to live your life?

#3 Assign your *Vision*—What do you *want*?

#4 Reinforce *Purpose*—*Your answer to, "What's the point?"*

#5 Live the *Commitment*—What are the activities you are committed to doing to align you with your purpose?

#6 Establish *Criteria*—Establishing your crystal-clear criteria for your next job or desired position

#7 Seek *Differentiators*—An exercise of drilling into what makes you… you.

#8 Send in the *Negotiator*—Once the seven previous steps are complete, you are in the power position. Learn what to do when you have 4 job offers (like I did).

The Truths can be grouped into three categories:

Category A: Truths #1-3—*Being Aware*
Category B: Truths #4-6—*Being Active*
Category C: Truths #7-8—*Being Assertive*

Each chapter gives you a description of the Truth, an example of how it works, an example of how it applies in my life or for a client, maybe a story or two, then the chapter will be concluded with what I call a "Sanity Check Station." This check station is a question you can ask yourself to know if you are living in that Truth.

In my workshop, I draw the analogy between this paradigm shift and doing the laundry. You must start with some clean clothes, so first we wash the clothes to get a clear head and clean slate. You are ready for change when you having nothing left to wear—you start reading this book—and you are loading up the washer with all your clothes.

After some self-reflection while the clothes are in the dryer and after they are dry, I am going to throw all the clean clothes at you to sort, fold, and put away. On some days, the load may seem supergiant, and on other days, the load may seem lighter.

After the clothes are sorted, the order in which you fold them is really important. This process is to be done in a serial format, without skipping around. Each Truth builds on the other. Take the time you need to absorb each Truth before moving on to the next pile.

Back to You

It is your choice in how you view the load, but you must trust that if they are sorted, folded, and put away, you will show up in a spectacular outfit! And the most beautiful thing about the process? No one can tell you what to wear, or when you need to get dressed.

A job is like any personal relationship. When things get bad and you leave, life does not necessarily get better. It is when we realize what we are (and what we are not) willing to tolerate that a shift can occur. The truth is, patterns repeat themselves until the common denominator changes.

"Listening to your heart is not simple.
Finding out who you are is not simple. It takes
a lot of hard work and courage to get to know
who you are and what you want."
– Sue Bender

TRUTH # 1: FIX YOUR BELIEFS

"Tell yourself a better story. Then believe it."
– Jenny Krengel

Category A: Being Aware

The Undeniable Power of Belief Systems

The first time *I remember* getting in my head with self-doubt, and being completely confused about "what was wrong with me" was when I was about 16 years old. My boyfriend "Charlie" consistently lied to me and cheated on me. He would be fun, charming, and kind when it was just

27

us together and with his family, then in front of our peers, he would act like I didn't exist. Okay, so I was not capable at the time of the best choices, but I would ask myself, *"What did I do? What is wrong with me? Why would he do that?"* But I never had the guts to ask *him* those questions. And why *did* I stay?

I was told growing up, "Children are to be seen, *not heard."* My parents' generation were the masters of sweeping everything under the rug. If you don't talk about the problem, or the weakness, "Presto! It does not exist!" The David Blaine style of parenting.

I was also told I needed to behave a certain way, wear certain clothes, and be the way others wanted me to be because I might embarrass my mom in front of her family.

For the first 17 years of my life, I was routinely shown that daily life, money, and relationships are a struggle. Nightly fighting between my parents on the other side of the thin wall required a box fan to whir away the worry. To this day I still have white noise going strong on my bedside.

And guess what I created throughout my 20s and into my early 30s?

Silent struggle.

What does silent struggle look like? Never speaking up for myself. Consistently feeling like something was wrong with me, and feeling completely out of alignment.

It feels like being a muzzled dog on a retractable leash. "Come here... no go away...come back... okay you can wander... But don't open your mouth and bark... someone might think you are a b***."

It is exhausting and draining.

For some reason I did not *believe* I was worthy of better treatment. But along with the silent struggle, I also knew that I *was* loved, and that my parents did their best with what they learned, and that their intentions were good. They told me I was loved, and I gained special skills from the chaos. As I got older, making sense of it gave me understanding, acceptance, and gratitude.

As far back as I can remember, I had this fearless fire in my belly to *do* stuff. I would try almost anything that might be considered fun because if I saw it was *possible*, I *believed* I could do it, too. I have an older brother who is 17 months older than I, and I remember always looking up to him and wanting to keep up with him in athletics and whatever mischief he was up to. He and my dad called me, "Me too"!

TRUTH #1 FIX YOUR BELIEFS

What is a Belief?

Beliefs are the survival system for our life's journey, and the core of every decision we make. Some decisions are conscious, and some are unconscious. When we keep repeating the same patterns, and live the definition of insanity by doing the same thing over and over without different results, most likely it is our beliefs that we have to blame. Our beliefs put us on the hamster wheel and drive us to exhaustion. Our beliefs also help us find the most incredible job we could have ever imagined. Our beliefs can help us soar, and they can tank us.

Beliefs are everything we have learned in our lives to cope and survive. They are how we have wired our brains over years of repeated behaviors, and they are rules we have learned either from our childhood, from experience, or by making interesting assumptions that may or may not be true.

I am not a neuroscientist, but I have studied the subject, read countless books, and have had some formal education on the topic. People and behaviors fascinate me, so I guess that is why I chose a degree in psychology. Psychology attempts to continually answer the question "Why?" when it comes to behaviors and mental health.

We can be happiest in life when we focus on our own "why" and understand why we believe what we believe, then question those beliefs. Adopt the beliefs that are working, and discard those that are not.

It is never our job to try to figure out someone else, how they can change, and what their motivation or belief system is. We can guess, but I do believe the definition of self-torture is this:

Wishing anything other than yourself will change.

This attitude was how I found peace during the last election cycle. We will *all* drive ourselves crazy trying to understand where someone else is coming from. So like the funny Buddha photo I see on Instagram:

Types of Beliefs:

As mentioned in the previous chapter, there are two types of Beliefs: living beliefs, and disabling beliefs. The disabling beliefs hold us back, and living beliefs are those that let us fly. Beliefs are first adopted from our family of origin (work ethic, money, religion, politics, love, acceptance, etc.), then over our lifetime we filter, refine, and change, based on how the belief system is serving us. Key to note: a belief is just something we have *learned or adopted*, so understanding how beliefs serve us is critical to being mindfully aware in Truth #1.

In this process, we have to brain-dump every belief we can think of before we can start figuring out how to sort them out into types (laundry exercise!).

Examples of some my beliefs—not sorted—(many of these I learned from my family of origin):

1. Plan your work; work your plan
2. *See no evil; speak no evil; hear no evil
3. Don't talk; don't trust; don't feel
4. *All things in moderation
5. Chaos is to be expected, so create it if it is not present
6. Treat others as you wish to be treated
7. Money comes and goes

Out of this entire list of some of my beliefs, which ones serve me well? Only two. The ones that I consider living beliefs are number 1 and number 6. The two with the asterisks may seem innocent enough on the surface, but the way in which I *learned* them is to always be in denial (we don't see things, we don't hear things, and we don't say anything). The general intention of the saying is good, but that is not how it was taught to me.

The other asterisk, "all things in moderation," is well intentioned, but I've always felt like I had to keep a lid on things. If I felt the urge to experience something and get excited and be my free spirit, I would hear that belief. *Don't be too much this... don't be too much that...all things in moderation. Don't be a spectacle. Don't really be yourself if it is too much for someone to handle.*

Once you get rid of some old beliefs that are not serving you, and adopt new ones, amazing things will start happening for your peace of mind.

Let's Talk Money:

This one is fun. How about this belief: money is the root of all evil, or you can't buy happiness, or money can't make you happy. Oh, my. Are you ready to unpack? Do you buy any or all of these beliefs? If you do, you probably should put the book down now and continue to stay in your place of struggle and want.

What did you learn from your family of origin about money? Did you learn:

- To be dependent
- To be risk averse
- To be too risky
- To be chaotic, inconsistent

I want to be clear on this again: The *only* time in my career trajectory where I was focused on making money was to pull myself above the poverty line.

Money is a tool to help others, money is a gift to educate, and money funds experiences. Until you get a grip on the true meaning of money, you will struggle. I promise.

We get what we expect, people. I have my own issues and relationship with money that I face almost every day.

What we learn about money we learn first from a very young age. Here are some of my old beliefs about money:

1. Money comes and goes
2. Money is always there
3. Money is everywhere; if other people have it, so can I
4. Be thrifty, because saving is the right thing to do because my husband says it is
5. I learned that I should save money, but that means I live later. I want to live now
6. I am not worried about money
7. Work can be a struggle, but when I struggle I make money
8. I feel guilty making more money than other people

There can be "good" and "bad" found in every one of these. I had to ask myself the question: How well were my beliefs serving me as an employee and as a wife?

I have adopted one single belief about money, and it is serving me better than my wildest dreams! I will share my single belief about money when we get to the chapter on purpose.

Weeding the Garden:

I came up with this term when I realized how much stress I can strip back when I got in touch with my belief system. I was driving down the road and pictured a rose garden that was blooming. And when I saw the rose garden, there were no weeds, no bugs, nothing prohibiting the growth of the beautiful and fragrant flowers. So I asked myself, "Jenny, what or who are the weeds in your life? How can we eliminate the power they have been having over your growth?"

> *"Weed your garden and plant promises."*
> – **Jenny Krengel**

Being process oriented, I tried out a process and it worked. This was a highly personal exercise for me, and it was the first step in my process. What makes the process even better is that it was validated by a researcher at the University of Texas who was highlighted in the book by Brene Brown, *Daring Greatly*. This process uses writing.

Step 1: Shedding the Shame: Write down everything in your life you have ever felt embarrassed or shameful about. Write until you can't think of one more thing you could possibly apologize for or reveal about yourself. Write down secrets you have kept in your vault of shame, probably your whole life. Don't read it again—those memories do not deserve one ounce of thought or energy. Past events steal your joy. Don't choose to repeat them.

Step 2: Identify your *role* in your family of origin. What role did you play in your family? Were you ultra responsible? Were you the "baby"? Were you given no discipline so you could run off the rails? Know your role and how you believe you are playing your role today.

Step 3: Try new boundaries with your family of origin. If you have no parents, or brothers or sisters, examine how your role might be playing out with personal relationships.

Beliefs are all about awareness and wanting to live a different story. What do you believe, in all areas of your life?

My client Ann Marie believed she did not deserve to make more money. She told herself that making $36,000 a year was "enough," and she got used to the struggle. She told me she felt guilty for wanting to make more money and that her friends (who were all in the same financial boat) would make fun of her for having bigger dreams.

When I asked her what she wanted money for, she told me she wanted to make other people's dreams come true— like Oprah. She loved the idea of extreme generosity and helping others.

When we talked about Ann Marie's vision for herself, she never had "making more money" on the list. So one day I told her, "I know why you aren't making more money. It's because you have never made that a purpose. You feel guilty. How can we change your belief about money?"

Ann Marie made a conscious choice to shift her belief system and shed the shame. Within a year Ann Marie shifted her belief about money, and she doubled her salary. She has freed herself from a disabling belief and continues to reap the rewards of a climbing income.

What You Can Do:

Last summer, road construction was being done on my street, and there was a section of the road that was closed. That meant that when I wanted to turn right out of my driveway, I had to turn left, and use an alternative route. This rerouting went on for about six months until one day they finally opened the road. Even though I knew the road was open, on three occasions I automatically turned left out of my driveway—which was the wrong direction—out of habit. So I had to go down the road a bit and turn around. Sometimes I just kept going the other route because I was lazy and didn't want to turn around. I realize this is a simple example with no consequences, but our neural pathways are ingrained and connected to automatic behaviors—until we become keenly aware and change the pattern. Which direction do you want to turn out of your driveway?

Action: Brainstorm what your beliefs are, and start to modify what you tell yourself. Start adopting your own rules, and live by them, with truth, integrity, and respect for others. It takes 45 days to rewire our brains to live new habits, creating new outcomes.

Sanity Check Station #1: When you find yourself in a situation where you are telling yourself something (a belief), ask yourself: "What makes this belief *true*?" Then challenge the belief, and either use it, or lose it and then make up a new one.

What I'm Going to Do

TRUTH # 2: EMBODY YOUR VALUES

*"Aligning every choice you make with your values
is a dart hitting the bullseye of the heart."*
– Jenny Krengel

Category A: Being Aware

The Ugly Side of Being Out of Alignment:

My habits of serving others and caring about what everyone else wants, thinks, or feels, drove me to what I know, for me, was a nervous breakdown in early 2015.

After leaving a 20+ year career in high tech, I was somehow the co-owner and head operator of a retail store, and I hated it. I was the voluntary primary care-taker for an unstable mother at the time. I was worried about her on a daily basis—fighting her, plus battling her legal, financial, personal, emotional, and physical calamities. She was in the throes of recovering from near-death on Christmas Eve, and the situation was complicated and overwhelming.

Pressure was mounting and nothing could have prepared me for the moment I was on the floor of a filthy warehouse after falling off a ladder and hitting my head on some f*** box that wasn't supposed to be where it was. It was February and it freezing cold in there, and I was trying to climb through a tiny internal window because an access door was mistakenly locked. It was a comedy of errors, but I wasn't laughing.

I was going mad—losing my mind. I snapped, unlike anything I'd ever experienced before. I was crying, screaming, hitting the walls, and kicking everything in sight. What was most disturbing: I was planning my escape to never be found again.

At that moment I did not want any part of my seemingly beautiful life. I was down 30 pounds and healthy, had my "perfect" house in the "perfect" neighborhood, the most patient, loving husband on earth, money in the bank, and a brilliant daughter who is the love of my life. But I was resentful, broken, and joyless, and I needed to get fixed. Fast.

That moment I knew it was time to say *enough is enough*, and I drew a line in the sand. I grabbed back my boundaries in an instant. I told my husband/co-owner of the business, "I quit, effective immediately. You can figure it out."

I had to get my sanity back. My fuse had been 49 years long, and the dynamite was ignited. I needed to figure out my real worth, my career, and my next move. Not what anyone else wants. Not what anyone else thinks. Not what anyone else needs. But what do I want?

I gave everything and everyone the stiff arm and said to myself, "My turn to take care of Jenny." No blaming—I've chosen my life. But I knew I was completely out of whack and *needed* to get back to myself. This was not a vacation request, but a full-on transformation that had to take place. Re-set.

TRUTH #2 EMBODY VALUES

What is a Value?

If our beliefs are the survival system for our journey, our values are the compass.

Values should be consistent and reliable, and they are ours alone.

In their simplest form, values are your heart's wishes and desires for how you want to live your life. Without knowing, adhering to, and *living* our values, the path becomes blurry, confusing, and the wheels can fall off the wagon.

Think about what really makes you mad, pushes your buttons, or gets you upset. In most cases, one of your values has been violated. On the other hand, when you are feeling the most joy and freedom, your values are being honored.

Types of Values

In my training, when I first did the values exercise (choosing less than 10 from a comprehensive list of redeeming qualities any sane person would covet), there were some values that stood out more clearly than others. At the time, I felt like I really connected with words like "safety," "efficiency," and "responsibility." Then there were words/values that did not really connect with me, like "holistic living" (woo-woo), "privacy," or "self-care." I was feeling happy about my values and was feeling, "*Okay, this makes sense! I value efficiency.... I am not crazy.... This is a good thing.*" Classic rationalization. I sat with this new knowledge, and something wasn't sitting right.

Then I asked myself a magical question that changed my life: "If Lily (my daughter) were grown up, and she had to remember her mom, what would she say?"

And it struck me like a lightning bolt. I had ZERO desire for the person I cared for most in this world to remember me as "efficient" and "responsible." I wanted her to remember me as adventurous, fun, dependable, honest, and authentic.

So right then and there I made a decision to live into how I wanted my daughter to remember me. I call this conscious choice an IVS: Intentional Value Shift.

It is the process, of letting go of old values and adopting new ones, that supports happiness and growth, not control. There are two types of values: conscience-based values and fear-based values.

Conscience-based values are values that rely only on me; they are things that solely depend on my behavior or desires.

Fear-based values are values that are based on disabling beliefs (efficiency = I must have control), or dependent upon external forces (recognition = someone has to honor me).

Making Values a Verb:

We see companies, churches, and organizations post their values on the wall, and simply doing the exercise is valuable. But we need to take the exercise a step further. Values need to be an action. We need to decide what the values *mean* to us.

Example of values with attached meaning:

VALUE	VERB
Fun	Finding humor and laughter in the simple things
Integrity	First being honest with myself and with others
Courage	Doing something anyway even if I feel afraid

When you feel like a train running off the tracks, you are likely out of alignment with your values. This step will help you remain true to yourself, and if you create an acronym to remember them and live them, every decision you make will become easier, and you will feel more centered.

My client Vivian was consistently getting frustrated with a co-worker she felt was trying to sabotage her. One day she was explaining to me how the co-worker had an agenda, and how she felt he was trying to make her look bad.

I asked her, "What is your core value that keeps getting violated?"

She answered, "Integrity. My number one value is integrity."

Me: "How can you stay true to your values without allowing him make such an impact on you and your emotions?"

Vivian: "Hmmmmm. Well I guess what he does doesn't really matter, and if I live in integrity and know my truth, then he can't really impact me or my performance."

Exactly!!

What You Can Do:

I have a litmus test for values that may not be 100% bulletproof, but it has served me and my clients well. Once you believe you have settled on your values, after you have taken some time to identify them, live with them, and make your IVS, here is a question you can ask yourself: "*If I were on a desert island, would my values serve me?*" If you had to rely *only* on yourself to either get off the island to survive, or make yourself comfortable while you were waiting to be rescued, how would your values serve you?

Understanding and living your values in a meaningful way will be life-changing for you and everyone around you.

Every day you are given choices to decide what it is you want, and your beliefs and values will give you your answers. For free. Will you figure out a way to move away from them and stay "safe," or will you take the path to move toward them?

When you identify your values and *live* them you will make a significant shift not only for yourself, but for everyone close to you in your life.

Sanity Check Station #2: Ask yourself: "How do I want _____ to remember me?" Fill in the blank with the most meaningful person to you right now. If you are struggling at work, maybe the question is, "How would I want my boss to remember me?" Live your values—represent them well.

What I'm Going to Do

TRUTH # 3: ASSIGN YOUR VISION

"The courage you have is more
powerful than the skills you lack."
– Jenny Krengel

Category A: Being Aware

In Touch with a Vision:

Recently I saw a motivational saying that was something along the lines of, "Dreaming is a form of planning." I love it when I see a philosophy that aligns with what I think and feel; it validates me and I get a free pass off the crazy-train. The concept of the world needing "dreamers who do" is spot-on. I believe the ability to have a dream or a vision is a gift. When I was a young girl, and when I was a single woman before marriage and child, the first thing I would do in the morning was to spend time staring at the ceiling, just thinking. Dreaming, really. Sometimes for only a few minutes, but oftentimes for more than an hour. I would turn on some music, and I could choreograph complex routines by seeing them in my head. I could literally *feel* the music, and put myself in the scene. The dancers entered the stage at specific times. I could see their costumes, and count out the parts. Everyone had a place and a part, and I knew where all the pieces went. The production was beautiful, calming, inspiring, and flawless.

Dreaming *is* a form of escape or a form of planning. The magic is finding a way to balance the two, and compromising to make our dreams (or visions) real. I believe I am closest to God when I am in the zone with a vision.

In my career, the least amount of money I ever made was when I had the vision to start my own software company, Dream Jobs Inc.

When I had the idea, at the time I felt that it was my calling, and I was the happiest I've ever been in a job. Ideas flowed, work was effortless, and I felt like I was unstoppable. The idea was great! Customers were buying! Investors, friends, and family were more than supportive! But it was not meant to be. The market had different plans. At the time, my husband worked at Lehman Brothers, so his job went away. There we were. No job, no business, and no income.

But we had faith. We relied on our beliefs and values at that vulnerable time in life. Our core family values embraced personal responsibility, healthy choices, and trusting the process.

Thanks to my husband's financial foresight, we had liquidated equity in our home, sold it just in time, and rented a home for ultimate flexibility. We had no idea what would happen next. Then we had a vision.

What if we opened our possibilities? What if we separated from financial attachment, and trusted options that are presented to us? We did that. We went all-in with our savings on a business venture, and in a period of three years, we relocated to another city, sold a business, and a former employer rehired me to develop an unknown territory—and we bounced back, better than ever.

I owe this vision to my husband, because at the time I was so focused on reviving the dream I had for my company that I would have definitely gone down with the ship when the financial services market collapsed in 2009. And that would have been okay if I were single, but I wasn't. And we had a child.

TRUTH #3 ASSIGN YOUR VISION

What is a Vision?

If our beliefs are our survival system, and our values are our compass, then our vision is our destination.

A vision is what you want for your life. Before you start a job search or career, it is critical to answer the question, "What do I *want* for my life?" The answer to this question will give you direction, peace, and a roadmap to what financial resources you need to accomplish your dream or vision.

Working with clients, I have found this question to sometimes be overwhelming and too big. When I work with a business I want the CEO to tell me what they want in the next three years, and I have found that timeframe works well for career seekers too.

A three-year window does not feel so big. It is manageable and doable for us dreamers.

Some life coaches or gurus will use the question, "When you are 100 years old what will you have regretted not doing?" or, "What is your legacy?" I don't like the 100-year-old question because, despite the crappy or challenging things that have happened in my life, I do not regret one choice I've made... other than not staying in Los Angeles when I was 21 years old to dance with The Lakers Girls and make MTV videos with Paula Abdul, Tina Landon, and Teri Hatcher. I believe there is a season for all things.

I could answer the 100-year-old question, "I regret that I never danced on Broadway." Okay, I logically know that, in this season in my life, I am not going to ditch my husband and daughter and sacrifice all the other things that are important to me to go dance on Broadway. I will find a local theater or something else to fulfill the feeling I want from dancing on Broadway.

I try to balance my dreamer side with my practical side on a regular basis. That's why I like the three-year rule. I can promise you that—at or around three years away from my daughter graduating from high school and leaving home—"dancing on Broadway" will probably become one of my visions. For the sake of loving my family more than that vision, I am happy to shelve that one for a while and wait for the right season. I am not a proponent of complete selfishness for the sake of pursuing visions and dreams.

Getting to your Vision:

After the unforgettably traumatic events of being way out of alignment happened to me while I was parent-care-taking and running a tactical gear store, I knew I needed to get back to me. The three things *I wanted most* were to experience joy again, find my purpose, and to feel free.

In addition to these feelings I wanted to get back, I wanted some other things.

For example:

- Solo retreat—get away somewhere by myself (I was feeling strangled)
- A bad ass car (yes, this is true—I love the smell of a new car—and I feel pretty)
- Not to feel judged by others (we do this to ourselves)
- To accept my body (linked to self-judgment)
- Loving work again—feeling like my work matters
- A fantastic lake house
- Quit doubting myself (lack of confidence)
- Help develop people

This is a long list of things to want. One of my gifts is the ability to distill complex ideas and information into bite-sized pieces, and I love helping other people get clarity this way.

After making my list (the above bullets are only about half of the items that were on my list) I needed them to rest. I needed to sit with them and, like the laundry, I needed time to sort them out.

Here is what I realized: When I fixed my beliefs and intentionally started living my values, three things happened. 1) Like Dorothy in the Wizard of Oz, I had my ruby red slippers on and the ability to go home the whole time. I have always had joy and freedom and a sense of purpose. 2) Those "wants" go away when you identify and *live* the beliefs and values, and create a vision for your life. 3) I spoke one day with the wise Rich Litvin, and he said, "If you really wanted what you say you want, you would have it." WOW! That advice was mind-blowing to me. I believe that to be absolutely true. All of us have exactly what we want. And we are always exactly where we want to be. (Despite the lies and excuses we give ourselves.)

Through my distillation process I narrowed down my three-year vision to two things:

1. I want to give my daughter the gift of traveling the world and experiencing how other cultures live.
2. I want to work from anywhere in the world and make money while I sleep.

Notice these sentences start with "I want…." Now I am on a mission to make these things happen.

What You Can Do:

Brainstorm ALL the things *you think you want* in life. Don't judge them. Just write them down.

You can distill your list to create your vision statement this way: What *matters most* to me? Or, what is the best gift I could give _____ (daughter, son, mother, sister, nieces, nephews, friend)? Or, what will allow me to live the life I want?

Sanity Check Station #3: Ask yourself: "What do I really want for myself? If I don't have it, do I really want it?"

What I'm Going to Do

TRUTH # 4: REINFORCE PURPOSE

"Finding purpose is not a chase. It is a giant pause.
It is slowing down to pay attention."
– Jenny Krengel

Category B: Being Active

The Seemingly Giant Question: What's My Purpose?

B elieve it or not, we are on the homestretch of sorting out our Truths. This chapter and the following chapters get easier as we work on our awareness from the inside out and apply action. Taking action is easy, right? Yes. Nod with me, now. Believe it.

In this chapter I am combining the three Truths that fall into the category "Being Active." Since your laundry is clean, and it has been sorted, it is time to neatly fold the laundry, with care. You are *taking action to make things happen!*

Finding "purpose" is a common place for people get stuck, and I believe we need to trim down to exactly what purpose really is. "Being stuck" is another convenient way for us to talk ourselves *out* of action. "Stuck" is a destination we choose, whether we want to admit it or not. A word I have removed from my vocabulary is overwhelm. Feeling overwhelmed is simply an emotional state of shutting down because it is our brain's way of tricking us into the belief that we cannot handle a situation. The reality is we have built up our use of that feeling over time, reinforced the feeling, and then used it as an excuse to stay stuck in avoidance. It is a fear-based emotion that is a result of pressure we put upon ourselves. Usually the pressure has to do with something we make up about time, and/or getting a "perfect" result. This behavior is tied into a belief system, and I am addressing the topic of overwhelm here, because that constructed feeling causes inaction. We are starting the section on *Being Active,* so throw the word overwhelm in the trash.

TRUTH #4 REINFORCE PURPOSE

What is a Purpose?
Purpose is not something to be chased. "Purpose" is a single word for "What's the point?" I will never be able to explain this pathology—maybe it is my creative spirit, or the remains of some old trauma hidden in the sub-conscious—but the

word "goal" makes my chest tighten up and feel brief panic. There you have it. We are supposed to be "goal-oriented." Write down your goals. Make it your goal. Ughhhhh! I literally feel constricted when I use that language, so for this book and for your bite-sized learning, we are going to replace the word goal with the word purpose.

Sometimes it is not worth trying to figure out why we are the way we are. Accepting how we are can be a beautiful and calming gift we give ourselves, especially when our intentions are good and we are not hurting anyone else. "Unpacking" the meaning behind a problem or a situation can be helpful, but it can also become a heavy burden we put on ourselves. Sometimes we need to keep the suitcase packed and just enjoy the stay. There are days when unpacking does no good other than to torture ourselves into so much self-introspection that the exercise becomes fruitless. Give yourself a break, and in the end, I have to believe that no harm on this planet will be done by replacing the word goal with the word purpose.

Purpose in Action

Up to this point you have become aware of your beliefs and values, and you have thought about your vision and what it is you want for your life. Let's go back to my 30s when my vision was to love my work and to buy my first home.

As I was sorting out how I was going to do this, I found a company I wanted to work for, and decided that was my purpose. *My purpose (goal) for the next 12 months is to get a job at XYZ Software Company.* Your purpose is in definitive language. You are going to make that happen. Remember, your purpose can change. It depends on how big you want to make your vision, and you can have more than one purpose. I currently have four purpose statements that I love, feel entirely connected to, and that have been solid for going on a year now. I do not see them changing for years, although I may add to the list.

In chapter three, I mentioned that today I have one belief about money, and it has released my feelings of guilt and my wacky perceptions about making a lot of money. It is one of my purpose statements: *My purpose is to fund experiences for myself and others.* With this intention as my compass, I allow myself to be in a place of service without the nonsense of guilt getting in the way.

My client Caroline had a vision of making a six-figure income so she could travel the world, and donate her time and money to helping child literacy. She had never made more than $60,000, and she felt constrained in her current position as a project manager. She always felt like she had so much more to offer but didn't feel like she was qualified to try another role in the high tech industry.

After going to one of my workshops, Caroline decided her purpose was to change careers and to reach for a role that was way outside of her comfort zone. She wanted to try sales!

She shifted her belief system and told herself she was, not only trained and capable, but also that she had NO doubt she was a terrific candidate to try software sales.

Then she made a radical decision. Even though she had 15 years of work experience and an impressive "Director" title, Caroline decided she would take a step back financially to invest in herself and take an entry-level position that would lead her to her aspirational role. She was upfront in the interview process, and she is on her way to a new career by switching gears, getting uncomfortable, setting pride aside, and aligning with her values, vision, and purpose!

What You Can Do:
1. If you find yourself saying you are overwhelmed, acknowledge you are making up that feeling.
2. Write down the goals, purpose statements you want to tackle, say in the next year. You can use a shorter timeframe if you want. Like a recipe instruction, set the purpose statements aside; we will come back to them.
3. Give yourself permission to change your purpose as it suits what you want, and know that it is a dynamic process. Life happens along the way as we make plans!

Sanity Check Station #4: Ask yourself: "What matters to me most today?"

What I'm Going to Do

TRUTH #5 LIVE THE COMMITMENT

—❧—

*"Scoring doesn't happen from
the sidelines. Play the game."*
–Jenny Krengel

What is a Commitment?

Some of us live our lives being a commitment-phobe. For a stretch between my mid-20s and mid-30s, I dated the same man off and on again for nine years. I went to see a therapist because my life just wasn't working the way I had envisioned. My intention for seeing the therapist was to figure out what was wrong with *him*. I was constantly getting mixed messages, and I needed some clarity.

On the surface, what a bad strategy that was! If a therapist, coach, consultant, (or whatever the service provider is) is actually good at what they do, they truly want you to be better off and actually *stop* seeing them. Steve-the-therapist was good! It took one question and one comment in our second session together to make a blinding light bulb go off in my head.

I had been lamenting with Steve-the-therapist about my view that, if *Joe would change* and finally commit to me, we would be happy ever after. We just have this *one* issue.

Then comes the hammer.

"Jenny, if you wanted to be married you would be. If for nine years you have dated someone who will not commit, who is the commitment-phobe?" BAM!

Speechless. Then he goes on to say, "He needs to look in the mirror, and you are standing right in front of him."

The truth is, he was actually saying the reverse to me, but he knew I would get out of the way of someone else faster than really examining what I needed to take a hard look into.

Commitment is the ability to be vulnerable to the actions it takes to arrive at the purpose.

"You can't (kinda) mountain bike."
— **Jenny Krengel**

For anyone who has ever mountain-biked, you know it is not a half-ass commitment. Snow skiing is the same way as you go down the mountain. If you don't commit, you are more likely to injure yourself because hesitation and doubt creep in. You are in or you are out.

In a personal relationship or job, this idea can be a trick. Commitment is not about being in at *all c*osts. In my long-term relationship, I was viewing commitment in an unhealthy way for me. I was in. I was going to stick it out.

But over time, if the mountain bike trail or ski trail never ended, the commitment would become exhausting and unsustainable. There must be a check point to determine when the level of effort you are putting in is commensurate with results.

The difference between healthy commitment and unhealthy commitment? In an unhealthy commitment, you are top-heavy on giving your all. In a healthy commitment, you are getting what you want out of the effort.

Commitment in Action

When I had the vision of loving my work and buying my first house, I had the purpose of going to work for XYZ Software Company. The next question became, "How am I going to get this dream job?"

So I started asking myself a bunch of questions: Who do I know at the company? No one. Is anyone I know acquainted with someone who works there? No. Have you ever sold client-server-enterprise-software? No. Why would they hire you, Jenny? Because I can sell. I love helping my customers, and this product is super badass!

Okay then. Let's do this.

My tenacity paid off by being connected to my core. I knew what I wanted for my life. It took close to a year to get this job, but I was in another job at the time where I was comfortable, working a lot from home, and able to pay my bills and live comfortably. I was happy, but not stretched. I wanted to be on fire and excited about what I was doing! I was hired by a man who believed in me, trusted me, and inspired me on a daily basis. And by the way, my resume did not match the job description or requirements.

What You Can Do:
If you want to get what you really want out of life and your career, you must be willing to commit. Commit in a healthy way.

There is no free lunch, and getting what we want requires a tenacious mindset. For those of us who may tend to lean in on the co-dependent side of the room by being people pleasers, living our Truths can *feel* selfish at first. I use the word selfish because I have used it in the past, and I hear my clients use that word when they are transforming their careers and lives. Throw the word selfish in the trash can with its cousin, overwhelm.

Don't believe the lie of "being selfish." If "being selfish" even occurs to you, you are not. The feelings and opinions of other people do not occur to truly selfish people, so that word is not in their vocabulary. Being selfish *is an action* of hurting other people intentionally through negative behaviors (lying, stealing, cheating) to get what you want.

Your commitment statement should start with the words, "I am committed to…, I am obsessed with…, or I am focused on…."

For example, your purpose and commitment statement should look something like this:

Vision: I want to love my work and buy my first house.

Purpose: My purpose for the next 12 months is to get a job at XYZ Software Company so I can make six figures.

Commitment #1: I am focused on understanding what it will take for me to get an interview.

Commitment #2: I am committed to researching more about software and technology so I can nail the interview.

Commitment #3: I am obsessed with figuring out a way to communicate why they should hire me.

Every day, our feelings and brain will try to trick us into staying in what is comfortable. I keep my vision, purpose, and commitment statements taped to my cabinet next to my desk. When I find myself getting sucked into helping somewhere where I am not needed, only attracted by the momentary buzz, or find myself thinking I can rescue a person or thing, I redirect myself and my behavior to my current vision for my life and career. Mystery solved. I feel super clear and super fulfilled! Plan your work and work your plan.

Sanity Check Station #5: Ask yourself: "What am I doing today? Will this task or action map to my vision and purpose?"

What I'm Going to Do

TRUTH #6 ESTABLISH CRITERIA

———✦———

"BE your own vibe."
–Jenny Krengel

What are Criteria?

I am consistently amazed when people go job searching and they can't articulate to me what they really want. I will ask, "What is important to you in a job?" And I get, "Hmmmmmm... that's a good question, let me think...."

Here is a common job-search process and the internal dialogue that accompanies:

1. Graduate from college with accounting degree. "Mom always wanted me to be an accountant. I guess I will get my degree in accounting. There will always be a job. It is a stable and safe career with a predictable path."

2. Attend PWC recruiting event because they are hiring with competitive pay and benefits. "I'm not really excited about sitting in a closet-sized room at a client's side conducting audits, but I will suck it up because it is what I need to do to make partner one day. This achievement *will make everyone* proud of me."

3. Get three job offers, and accept the one with the highest pay and that will not require moving. "I have no idea what to expect, but they like me, and this is good experience. I really want to relocate and know who my boss is going to be, but the money and benefits are good."

If this candidate had been clear about her beliefs and values, had constructed a vision for her life that was supported with a purpose, commitment, and criteria for her ideal job, the feelings of uncertainty and internal dialogue of justification and self-doubt would dissipate.

This anecdote is a true story that happened to a friend of mine in college. After ten years of this career she felt lost, burned out, and sold out. When she figured out how to get clarity and be true to herself, she exited that world gracefully and found another field on which to go play.

"A list is meaningless unless you check things off.
Which means you followed through."
– Jenny Krengel

Clarity in Action:

I am not expert on the law of attraction, but the concept works. My dear friend and business confidante Linda calls being aware and in-tune with everything that is happening in your life, "putting up your dog ears." She's one smart cookie, and I will never forget her giving me this advice.

I love this metaphor because the tendency is to walk through life on autopilot. Not paying attention to all the doors, windows, and avenues that are being opened and presented for us. Too much time is wasted being a victim and being confused about what to do next.

Lists are awesome! The best list I ever made was the one I made when I wanted to move out of the nine-year relationship and find a healthy commitment that would serve me and my needs. Identifying the criteria for my next relationship was critical to my awareness if I were going to keep my dog ears up and pay attention. I hired a coach, and she helped me through this process.

On a blind date, I actually got what I was looking for, and it scared me to death. If the universe had just delivered what I wanted, and when I got it I was scared, then what the hell is wrong with me? The truth is, nothing was wrong with me—I was in new territory. New territory scares us, and the tendency is to run or avoid that uncertain feeling, but we shouldn't let it stop us. In those moments of temporary fear, I have found that when I face the fear and do the opposite of what I *think* I should do, interesting and exciting things happen!

The ideal list brought me the best husband on the planet. My friends and family will agree. In no way is he perfect, but he is perfect for me.

When I was determined to get my job with XYZ Software Company I made a list. I knew what I wanted in a job, and I wrote down my criteria:

- Open a new territory—check
- Make a difference in a company with less than 100 employees—check
- Work from home—check
- Love my boss—check
- Feel passionate about the product—check
- Travel—check
- Learn the software business—check

This list is not comprehensive, but I wanted to give an example of the criteria I had established. Once I had my criteria established, my job hunt had become an *equally balanced* process of me interviewing them. I was not afraid. Because I was focused, clear, and prepared, once I got the interview, the process was smooth as silk.

My client Suzanne is a terrific example of being aligned with criteria. Suzanne had mostly worked in a big corporate environment, but after working together with me, she felt she could best serve with her gifts and talents in a start-up company. She wanted to make a difference at work!

Money was not a driver for Suzanne, as she was used to a six-figure income. But she got very clear about her workplace, her boss, her environment, the products that the company was selling, and her teammates. She *knew* exactly what she wanted from her job. Then the universe delivered.

After designing the perfect job, and being offered the perfect job, guess what happened? Suzanne freaked out! She got exactly what she wanted; now what?

This phenomenon is common, so watch out for this blind spot. There was a certain amount of anxiety and fear in getting what she wanted, so over the course of a couple of weeks, she worked through her old patterns of self-doubt and overwhelm.

Together we kept her on-course by fixing her old beliefs, embodying her values, assigning her vision, reinforcing her purpose, living the commitment, and establishing her criteria!

What You Can Do:

Make a list of ideal criteria for your job. Simple. It's yours. It's what you want. It's your Truth #6.

Sanity Check Station #6: Brainstorm and ask yourself: "In a company, job, or boss, what are my must-haves and can't stands?" Get clear. Write down your criteria.

What I'm Going to Do

TRUTH # 7: SEEK DIFFERENTIATORS

"You cannot be yourself until you know yourself."
– **Jenny Krengel**

Category C: Being Assertive

The best product you will ever carry is you. You probably would not have made it to this point in the book if you did not believe that too. As we go out in the job world to make our mark… to matter… and to make a difference for ourselves, our families, our employers, and our co-workers, do you know what makes you, you?

If you don't know why someone should hire you, then you probably should not be looking very hard for a job. If you can't give someone a reason "why" they should hire you, then one of three things happens:

1. You continue to struggle on the outer edge of the Career Mastery Model™, busy executing tasks and busy with activities and shooting in the dark.
2. You get another job and experience the same frustration, and you jump from the fire to the frying pan.
3. You win the job lottery and get very lucky, based on statistics that are not stacked in your favor.

When I was laser focused in my work, it was easy to differentiate myself because I was honest and had a genuine desire to produce.

One of my favorite examples of how I used differentiation to make a big deal happen was when I wanted to sell to a major oil company based in Houston, Texas.

I was working for a small start-up based in Richardson, Texas, selling a commoditized product, the un-sexy remanufactured toner cartridges, and the competition was fierce. Over a timespan of many months of trying to reach him, I had finally connected with the decision maker, and I wanted a meeting.

I miraculously got him on the phone (it is *not* a new thing that buyers don't usually pick up the phone), and he politely told me he had already made his decision on the contract, and it would be a waste of time to pursue any further.

I said to him, "You may have made your decision, but you haven't met me. I can help you. I know I can. I am different, and the company I work for is different. We may not do business together now, but I want to talk face to face so we can both decide if a working relationship would make sense one day. Would you agree to that?"

I guess he was in a good mood because he said yes. Like in the movie, *Dumb and Dumber*, in my head I was saying, "So there *is a chance*!"

My contact Rob was based in Oklahoma so I made the trip up. We got the contract. And this was no small account. The account blossomed into a multi-year, multi-million dollar relationship and one that I hold dear in memory to this day.

If you apply this same mindset and strategy to a job search, it works. The truth is I don't know that I have any magical differentiators, but I have always loved my customers and wanted to take care of them. Not all salespeople or employees can say that. But when you speak from the heart, let yourself be vulnerable and just talk your truth, the magic continues to happen.

What is a Differentiator?
I prefer the word distinguish to differentiate, but differentiation is a classic marketing strategy that works. When it comes to you as a candidate, I encourage you to figure out what it is that distinguishes you, because that word is about being special, and being special is more fun that just being different. Right?

When you are setting yourself up to look for a job, change your career, or move within the company you work for, you should know what distinguishes you from the rest of the sheep standing in line for the same job.

For the basis of this chapter, there are five categories of Market Differentiation, three of which we will apply to you as the "product," and the customer as the potential employer. I want to thank Mr. Graham McInnes for giving me permission to use his outstanding visual!

Source: Graham McInnes

For the purpose of this book and job hunting, only the ovals above the 40% line apply to the following examples.

Differentiation in Action:
Product Differentiation—If you are the "product" and someone is supposed to "buy" you, here are three questions for you to explore and be ready to answer:

1. What makes me unique? Perhaps you speak two foreign languages. Maybe you have an unusual life experience you can share.

2. What have I mastered? What could you speak about for 15 minutes or more without any notes? What could you teach someone else without any outside assistance?

3. What special skills or experiences do I have? Have you learned anything new recently? What skills could you put to use? Can you tell a story about how you helped Random Company grow from x to x?

Customer Service Differentiation—If the employer is the customer, and you want to provide outstanding service, answer these questions with confidence:

1. What promises can I make?—This might tie to your values. For example, you could say, "I may not be an expert at Excel *yet*, but I will promise I am dependable, and I will do what it takes to deliver what is expected of me."

2. What do I offer that is different?—Perhaps you are incredibly organized and you like to help others get organized. This is a gift you should offer.

3. How do I support the customer employer?—"Ms. Employer, please know that being resourceful is one of my core values. If there is a solution, I am committed to turning over all stones to find it."

User Experience Differentiation—This category happens to be my favorite because it is your way of producing connection, and an emotional feeling with your potential employer.

1. In my interview, how do I want the hiring manager to feel about me?—This is your opportunity to be vulnerable and maybe share some of your wishes and dreams for the future. Be interested in your potential co-worker or boss. Get curious about what makes *them* happy.

2. What does my employer need?—Here is your opportunity to dig into what problems lie below the surface. Sure, you are being interviewed for a job, but what is most important to the hiring manager? How are they measured? How can you make your manager's light shine?

3. How will I be remembered?—This question should apply in your current job as well. In an interview, you can tell the employer, "I am committed to having a good attitude and being dependable, because if I ever leave this place or anything ever happens to me, I want to be remembered as an employee who cared." Whatever your words are in this message will be powerful, because they come from what you believe, and they are your honest truth.

What You Can Do:
In my workshop, I have my students text three people and ask them, "What am I great at?" Not only are the answers fun to

get, but they will give you insight into what others see in you. After you quit squirming, go do it. Tell them your instructor made you send this text. You will notice a theme. Use what you learn to your advantage!

Sanity Check Station #7: In addition to the questions earlier in the chapter: "What could I teach without notes? What common theme do I hear about my talents?"

What I'm Going to Do

TRUTH # 8: SEND IN THE NEGOTIATOR

———∿———

*"Self-torture is wishing anything
other than yourself will change."*
– Jenny Krengel

Category C: Being Assertive

I f a job or career search is all about marketing and sales, with you as the product, I want to reiterate the distinction between marketing and sales for the sake of emphasis.

To ease the pressure when you decide you are uncomfortable "selling" yourself, think of the activities this way: Marketing is information and data, and sales is a negotiation. If, on the front end of the job search, your mindset is to be first a marketer rather than a seller, does that feel better? Here's the key: There are sleazy marketers and sleazy sellers, and both buckets of sleaze drip in dishonesty.

Online businesses who push products or services without having a discussion or a negotiation with you are actually marketing to you. They are not selling. Transactions, quick closes, and putting on pressure is not selling. It is marketing. Pharma reps are not sales reps. They are live marketers. Car salesmen are not selling. They are live marketing. If something can be bought without human interaction (pharma works on referrals; cars can totally be sold on-line), then marketing is the function.

Sales or selling is when both people have established a trusting relationship with one another, and a negotiation occurs. Selling is *not* one-sided, and both interests are considered and respected. Marketing is one-sided until a conversation is required, then it becomes selling when a negotiation is mutually entered.

Have you ever bought anything, and afterward it felt yucky? Like a twinge of regret? I have felt like that when I knew a brilliant marketing person tricked me with a clever spin, shallow facts, or high-pressure tactics. It doesn't feel good. And transactional, eager-to-close-the-deal people are what gives sales and selling a bad reputation.

When you are in a job or career search, don't be the slick marketer, spinning facts and putting on the pressure. Don't be the commissioned sales guy at the retail store who follows you around like a puppy because he needs to get his quota and is feeling desperate. Take a professional sales approach.

Develop the relationship, build trust, and explore if the fit is right. You must believe the mindset that you are interviewing your potential employer as much as they are interviewing you. You will make yourself much more attractive that way. Just like dating.

What is Negotiating?

The word negotiation conjures up interesting feelings for people. When I ask, "How does the word 'negotiation' make you feel?" I get responses like, "win-win," or "compromise," or "give and take." Yes, exactly, that is what negotiation is, and Webster defines negotiate as:

- Obtain or bring about by discussion
- Find a way over or through

Daily life is a negotiation and so is a job search or career change. We look for ways to discuss and ways to find our way over or through the good times and bad.

Below is a simple graphic for my negotiation process. If you have Truths #1 through #7 nailed, negotiation is a walk in the park, and it will come naturally and with ease.

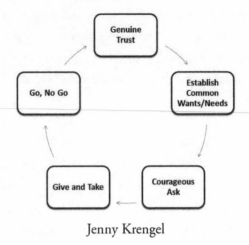

Jenny Krengel

Starting at the top with Genuine Trust and moving clockwise:

Genuine Trust—This step is based on your core values and the core values of your "opposition," or in most cases "collaborator." Opposition would be a term that would be applicable in a divorce or contentious action where a zero-sum game might be in play.

In an employer/employee interaction, the term collaborator more appropriately fits.

Understand what is most important to each party, and this approach will build trust. This is an alignment check.

Establish Common Wants/Needs—During the interview process, you will have covered this step. Before you get to an offer and may begin negotiating your employment, you will know your wants and needs based on your Truth #6—Criteria. During the interview process, it is important to understand your boss's or employer's wants and needs. Another alignment check.

Courageous Ask: In a negotiation, this can be the hardest part. You have to be honest about what you want and why. For example, your dream company makes you an offer, and the offer says nothing about the verbal agreement that was made to you to work remotely. You must not assume that you can or you cannot. Ask for clarity. You will not blow the deal. Whenever you are in doubt and something is not sitting right, ask. Ask, ask, ask. Do not hesitate.

Give and Take: Know what you are willing to compromise in an offer. Then negotiate. Stay true to your values, know where you stand, and keep an open mind.

Go, No Go: You must go into a negotiation knowing exactly what the deal breakers are. I had an employer I was negotiating with once, and I knew I would not work for less than a certain base salary I had in my mind. In my first interview, I made it known that if that salary took me out of the running, then so be it. But the interview process went forward and before I got the offer I reiterated my position on the salary. I received an offer for less than a) what I had communicated twice and b) what I *knew* another employee was making who happened to be male. I declined the offer, and I felt like trust had been violated and that no one listened to me. Those actions told me a lot about the culture, so it was a blessing in disguise.

Negotiations are not necessarily fluid, nor do they go in a perfect clockwise format. It is important to know that the more you are prepared on the front end by staying true to the previous 7 Truths, the more your negotiation will go effortlessly.

Negotiation in Action:

NEWSFLASH: Equal pay is not a unicorn or a yeti. Equal pay exists. It's called negotiation and production. The example I am going to walk through is for those of you who are not small business owners, have never employed or hired anyone, or are buying into the belief you are being treated unfairly by your employer who ostensibly pays your bills and is supporting the economy.

Here is an example of how equal pay works in everyday life, and *you* are the "employer" hiring an "employee." Negotiation in action.

You just had a minor car accident and the deductible is more than your repair. You don't want your premiums to go up, so you want to pay out of pocket for your repair. You post a request on Facebook and Instagram asking for anyone who can refer you to a good body shop for a straightforward repair job on the car.

You get lots of referrals from friends, and in fact, three people post on your social media pages with links to their own bodyshops. You get one from Bill's Body Shop, Sandy's Body Shop, and Joe's Body Shop. (This is like lots of resumes pouring in.)

You stop by each of the shops to check them out, ask some questions, see some work, and get a feel for how they do business. You want to ensure there's a vibe-match, and your process is pretty comprehensive. You let them all know you have a budget in the $600 range. (Kinda lame interview process, but it basically works.)

You let them know your requirements, then you ask for pricing from Bill, Sandy, and Joe. They each come back with different prices:

Bill = $500

Sandy = $600

Joe = $800

You want to choose the body shop you think will deliver the best value to you at the best price, but they each bring something a little bit different to the table. You put a lot of thought into what you really need, and end up selecting Joe for the work.

You call Joe and say, "Okay, I'm ready to get started, and am willing to pay you $600 based on the budget I have and some comparisons I've made in the made in the marketplace. I think that's a fair price."

Joe says, "Well, I am really busy right now, and at that price I just can't squeeze you in. I think I need to pass on the offer, but let me know if you need help in the future."

Okay, so on to the next candidate option. You're not sure about Bill since he is the lowest bidder, and he knew what the budget is so you have doubts thinking he may be a little desperate for the work. After all, after checking Bill's references his customers did not have great things to say about his work. In addition, his quality of work and communication style was not exactly a fit for you. He's okay, but you'll keep that option in your back pocket.

So you go to Sandy, and you feel comfortable offering Bill's lowest bidder price just to see if she would be willing to do the job for that price, and it is only $100 less than her bid. Why not ask? You will leave the choice up to her. You really like her. She had positive references, and you feel like she will do a good job.

You call Sandy and say, "Okay, I'm ready to get started, and I'd like to offer you $500 to do the work on my car." Sandy says, "Great! When do we get started?"

Sandy does the work. You are happy, Sandy is happy. Everyone gets what they needed.

Now… if Joe had taken the first offer for work at $600 ($100 more than Sandy accepted), would Sandy say she did not get equal pay and that she was treated unfairly? Did Sandy willingly accept an offer at a price she felt was fair? Sandy did not go back and renegotiate, but if she had, would you have been willing to pay her the higher price to do the same work? Probably. Or… if mid-work Sandy comes back and complains that she heard you offered Joe more, would you fire her? Probably not. Would Sandy do the work next time for you? Maybe, maybe not, but don't both of you have alternative options? Yes. This is America. Freedom rings and it rings loudly. If you don't like the system of economics and the job market, then go find something else to do.

Ladies and gentleman, the next time you take the victim stance that you are not being treated fairly, hold up the mirror and ask yourself what you need to do differently. If you do not believe you are getting fair pay, then find another job, or negotiate for yourself. Yes, I know, how *inconvenient*.

"*Ohhhh, a job search… ughhhh… I hate job hunting,*" you might say. But which do you hate more? Making a crappy salary and *feeling* undervalued (maybe you are, maybe you aren't), or actually taking the time and the effort to find an employer who will pay you more or value what you have to offer? It's your choice. Really.

If you want to have an honest conversation with someone who can make a decision about your pay, base your facts on your value, your contribution, your potential, and the competitive landscape. Understand whether or not you are easy to replace. Then *ask*!

Do your job in life. Take care of yourself, discuss what you want, negotiate, then make decisions that work for you. If you blame your employer, or the system, or the process… take your power back, get in the driver's seat, and go race on another track.

No one owes any of us anything. Not one single thing. Choose a better story and believe it.

What You Can Do:
When you have established your Truths: Beliefs, Values, Vision, Purpose, Commitment, Criteria, and Differentiators, I *promise* Negotiation becomes a function of just knowing when to walk away or to say "Hell, yeah, I am in!!"

We negotiate every day. Refining this skill in a high-pressure situation requires practice and fine-tuned skills. When I say high-pressure, I mean a hostage negotiation or peace talks—not employment. Practice, practice, practice. Practice the next time you want a better hotel room, or a better seat in the restaurant. It is fun to engage with people, and it is extra fun when everyone ends up with the happy meal they wanted!

Sanity Check Station #8: "What am I willing to tolerate, and why?"

What I'm Going to Do

CONCLUSION

"Ambition is achievement's soul mate. Action is the matchmaker that brings these affinities together so that sparks can begin to fly and we can set the world on fire."
— **Sarah Ban Breathnach**

Y ou started this book wanting something. You wanted to feel more connected to your work, you want to matter, you want to be more courageous in your communication, you want to make a difference, you want to love your work, and you probably want to make more money.

This process *works* if you decide to make the time, have the patience, and exert the tenacity to dig deeply. If you *truly* want to love your work and make more money, you must be willing to apply *your* Truths.

In working with clients in this transformation, even if you follow the formula, self-sabotage can come up in four basic flavors. The typical self-sabotage obstacles my clients run up against are:

Overwhelm: This feeling is a choice, and you must shift to a different feeling. We have programmed ourselves to *feel* overwhelmed, and this manufactured feeling keeps us in the safe place of denial, perfectionism, and self-doubt. To cure this paralysis, I call it "Replacing the O-rings." Replace the word Overwhelm with the word Opportunity. You can make an instant shift in your mindset by telling yourself that instead of feeling Overwhelm, I am choosing to see and experience Opportunity. "What is my Opportunity?"

Rationalization: "Well, my job isn't really that bad, and the money pays my bills." This is a dangerous place of inaction, and when you begin to say this to yourself, go back and visit the first three Truths.

Doubt: "Maybe it's just me. My boss is upset all the time, so I must be doing something wrong." If you are playing this song again, and going to work every day feels bad, examine how you are contributing to the dysfunction. Try to understand what is out of alignment. Better yet, ask your boss what the problem is, and fix it, or make another choice that will serve you.

Guilt: "I should be grateful to have a job." Maybe or maybe not. How much is being unhappy costing you? Are you really doing a good job for your employer? What could you potentially be doing to be happier, or to save more money for your vision to pay for your _____ (nephew's education, wedding, dream vacation, etc.)?

When these four self-sabotaging behaviors show up, explore Truth #1, and look at your belief system. What are you believing to be true or not?

In this book, I taught you the 8 Truths, what they mean, and how they apply to your job or career search. You can use this book as your guide, or you can reinforce what you've learned and make a minimal investment in my online training.

In writing this book for you, for my daughter, and for generations to come, I have these wishes for you:

- To be inspired to believe in yourself and your untapped potential
- To be honest with yourself first, in all your career endeavors
- To be adventurous and to live in trust over fear
- To know that the possible *is possible* for you, too

The 8 TRUTHS were *built in this order:* F-E-A-R-L-E-S-S, and you have learned how to:

#1 Fix *Beliefs*—How the beliefs we learn and develop impact our personal interactions. Our beliefs about money have unbelievable power over our behavior at work.

#2 Embody *Values*—How are you identifying and aligning with your heart's desire for how you want to live your life?

#3 Assign your *Vision*—What do you *want*?

#4 Reinforce *Purpose—Your answer to, "what's the point?"*

#5 **L**ive the *Commitment*—What are the activities you are committed to doing to align you with your purpose?

#6 **E**stablish *Criteria*—Establishing your crystal-clear criteria for your next job or desired position

#7 **S**eek *Differentiators*—An exercise of drilling into what makes you… you.

#8 **S**end in the *Negotiator*—Once the seven previous steps are complete, you are in the power position.

The Truths can be grouped into three categories:

Category A: Truths #1-3—*Being Aware*
Category B: Truths #4-6—*Being Active*
Category C: Truths #7-8—*Being Assertive*

Each chapter gave you a description of the Truth, an example of how it works, an example of how it applies in my life and for my clients, and a story or two. Then each chapter concluded with a "Sanity Check Station." This check station is a question you can ask yourself to know if you are living in that Truth.

From the words of one of my students who experienced this journey:

"Before Jenny's training, I often wondered why my work looked great on paper and to the world, but it didn't always feel so successful on the inside. There were great moments of pride, but there also were many moments where that wasn't the case, and I felt like I'd rather be more inspired by my work.

"I internalized this feeling and the thoughts that supported it and continued to climb the ladder of success by all outward measures.

"Having a framework in the course to identify my beliefs, and most especially my values, helped me to laser in on the core things that I had overlooked when approaching my work. Being able to articulate what I value and how those concepts translate to my vision for my work (and my life) has set me on a course where I can find momentum in my current role that will integrate what I do with who I am, and inevitably set me on the path to that dream role where what I do is that extension of who I am.

"Finding my purpose is something that emerges from within, based on what I truly value and the WHY I'm doing the work I do. I was pleasantly surprised to find I feel more satisfaction in my current role while preparing to take the next aligned step forward."

I want nothing more for you than to spread your wings, to live into your potential at work, and to live the beautiful life you dream about. You have the tools, and you *can* love your work and make more money!

With love and gratitude,

Jenny Krengel

SPECIAL THANKS TO YOU

When you are ready, please *take action* to reinforce these concepts you learned to craft the life and career *you* want! When you decide to invest in yourself, you also get to join a private online community where I show up live to help my students.

My special offer to you for being a book reader:

Go to www.8Truths.com to learn more about my small group and online training!

Hold on to your exclusive COUPON CODE: 8truths

For each online training sold, we donate one free training course to a career training pool for veterans, their spouses, and for single mothers who meet our scholarship criteria.

ACKNOWLEDGMENTS

I am eternally grateful for the people who have believed in me in my career, and for seeing things in me that I could not see for myself. I would like to give a heartfelt "thank you" and express deep gratitude for the following:

My mother Marion who taught me about work ethic and determination, and who carted me back and forth from so many jobs as a teen in that Ford Pinto. I have *no idea* how you made the time!

My father Jerry who was always a dreamer and my biggest cheerleader. I can only hope I inherited a tiny fraction of his sharp wit and creative genius.

I've worked with both my brother, Wiff Dedrick, and my sister, Jill Guarino, and they are both extremely talented, smart, and kind souls who have served as inspiration, love, and support in all my wacky adventures.

To my in-laws Ron and Elsa Krengel for the many hours of back-up child care, and the unconditional love they give to Lily, Russ, and me. I'm sorry for the handful of expressive cuss-words in this book.

Same to Erica Millard, Stephanie Colelli, Laura Rayburn, Kelly Sharp, and Kimberly Blackburn: my lifelong friends who have constant and unconditional love for me and my family.

To some wicked-smart and special former bosses and business mentors who always believed in me, inspired me to reach higher, and let me take chances: Jeff Odom, Andy Stack, Fred St. Amour, David Hydorn, Toby Richardson, Max Dodge, and Amir Husain.

My favorite teachers: Don Farmer, Cindy Russell, Professor Gerardo Okhuysen, and Dr. Angela Lauria for pushing me out of my comfort zone when I wanted to play small. My editor, Anna Paradox for seamlessly bringing your magic to my words.

A huge thank you to some of my dedicated and incredibly talented early students: Deanna Hendrickson, Monica Richardson, Angela Chow, Carol Hlavaty, Marie Cohen, Brittany Harmon, and Stacey Edwards. The world is at your feet, and you have everything you need for the fantastic journey you take yourself on!

My women-in-business colleagues, Linda Glass, Lise Hudson, Karen Manroe, Jill Hamlin, Allison Schickel, Shelley Pernot, Ramona Arora, Meredith Shapiro, Gina Budd, Megan Niles, Inga Valette, Kim Mineo, Pam Krengel, Heidi Brooks and Vanessa Fiola. You ladies are some kind of company! I love you all dearly, and I could not make it without your constant excitement, encouragement, and support. Plus my entire book launch team!

To Susan and Don Cox for your enduring love for me, and for keeping Christi's spirit alive through your heartfelt work; so faithfully serving those who are grieving.

To the Morgan James Publishing team: Special thanks to David Hancock, CEO & Founder for believing in me and my message. To my Author Relations Manager, Margo Toulouse, thanks for making the process seamless and easy. Many more thanks to everyone else, but especially Jim Howard, Bethany Marshall, and Nickcole Watkins.

And lastly, to my love, Russ. The one who told me I had talent when I didn't believe it, and the one who *always* loves me anyway. You make my chaotic world peaceful, and you bring the light to our family. Thank you for letting me be me. Probably the only one on the planet who could.

ABOUT THE AUTHOR

Finding her way out of economic stress in her twenties, Jenny Krengel figured out how to sell. She has bottled up her secrets to selling, and has developed a model and training course which teaches her students the 8 Truths a woman should know to find work she loves.

She dropped out of college at the age of 19 after being run over by a drunk driver that killed her roommate, but Jenny Krengel's attitude of survival and gratitude led her to a long and award-winning career in high tech sales, leadership, and entrepreneurship.

Leaving a six-figure income and the security of an eight year sales leadership role within a high-growth company in Dallas, Jenny eventually graduated from college with honors at the age of 32, with a self-funded BA degree in Psychology. She then returned to work in several software start-ups to use her talents to break into new territories, gain new clients, sell new products, and break sales records.

In 2005, Jenny took a year off work to enjoy her newborn daughter, and in 2006 she founded her own software company to help companies retain and re-capture talented women who had left the workforce to start a family. Her clients and prospects were in the financial services industry, and the market crash of 2009 devastated her company.

Keeping a positive mindset, trusting herself, honing her skills, and leaning on others, Jenny has refocused on her heart work: to educate and inspire women to live into their potential as happy, confident contributors in this modern workforce that needs their lights to shine.

She lives in Austin, Texas with her husband Russ, their daughter Lily, and their two dogs. It is Jenny's dream to play tennis at the US Open and to dance on Broadway—preferably on the same day.

Morgan James
Speakers Group

www.TheMorganJamesSpeakersGroup.com

We connect Morgan James published
authors with live and online events
and audiences who will benefit
from their expertise.